THE OFFICIAL MANCHESTER UNITED ANNUAL 2012

Written by Steve Bartram and Gemma Thompson

Designed by Brian Thomson

A Grange Publication

ISBN: 978-1-908221-30-8

Contents:

Hello and welcome to the 2012 Manchester United Annual...

Winning the league championship is always a great achievement. We made history and it is fantastic for the tradition of this club to be the most successful in English football, but we must not stop there and you can rest assured we won't.

Of course, we were disappointed not to end the campaign with two trophies after losing out to Barcelona in the Champions League final at Wembley. There has been good evidence over the last few years that we are a consistently good European team, but we were well beaten in the final by a side I regard as the best we have ever played. Quite simply we must do better and we will do our best to achieve that during the 2011/12 season.

As manager of Manchester United it's my job to keep the club moving forward. I'm not going to take it easy because we won the Premier League title. The main thing we want to do at this club is win. And I definitely feel this squad of players is well equipped to do that. We said goodbye to three great servants last season with the retirement of Gary Neville, Edwin van der Sar and Paul Scholes, but in Ashley Young, Phil Jones and David De Gea we have some exciting youngsters who I believe will develop into outstanding players for Manchester United over the coming years.

I hope they will blend in well with a group of players who have been brilliant for this club. They have always given everything out on the pitch and they deserve the success they have enjoyed. We played some excellent football at times last season and the players never failed to show their incredible hunger for success and refusal to accept defeat, which are both great qualities that have served us well and hopefully will continue to do so in the future.

But before looking forward, it is time to look back once more on last season's record-breaking campaign, including our trophy parade through Manchester. Plus, I hope you'll enjoy reliving the success of our young lads in the FA Youth Cup and reading all about our new signings. I also hope you have some fun along the way, of course!

Sir Alex Ferguson

REVIEW

Paul Scholes kicks-off the players' recollections of a record-breaking campaign, which began with a trophy for the Reds...

"Having lost the league by a point the previous season, we were really determined to go further and win the title back, so it was important to start the season well. It's always nice to beat one of your big rivals and pick up some silverware at the same time so we were delighted to win the Community Shield with a win over Chelsea at Wembley. It may only be a high profile friendly, but there's a trophy at the end of it and we wanted to win it. It was great to see Javier Hernandez on the scoresheet on his debut. He's such a threat, a real out-and-out goalscorer. He reminded me of Ole Gunnar Solskjaer the first time I saw him in training and he adapted to the pace of our game immediately. We looked strong in our first league game – a 3-0 win over Newcastle. They set their stall out and tried to make it difficult for us but we created chances and looked like we could score every time we went forward. I was pleased to net my 150th goal for the club away at Fulham, but ultimately the result was disappointing because we should have had the game wrapped up."

AUGUST

Sun 8	Community Shield
Mon 18	Premier League
Sun 22	Premier League
Sat 28	Premier League

August Stats

P:4	W:3	D:1	L:0
Scored: 11		Conceded: 3	
Clean Sheets: 2			

SEPTEMBER

Sat 11 **Premier League**

Tue 14 **Champions League**

Sun 19 **Premier League**

Wed 22 **Carling Cup 3rd round**

Sun 26 **Premier League**

Wed 29 **Champions League**

September Stats

P:6	W:3	D:3	L:0
Scored: 14		Conceded: 9	
Clean Sheets: 2			

United developed a worrying trend of letting leads slip but, as Jonny Evans recalls, still enjoyed a largely positive month in an action-packed September...

"Our away form became a talking point in the media. We'd dropped points at Fulham late on in August and we did the same at Everton. Over the past couple of years we've struggled to pick up points at Goodison Park; it's become a really tough place to go. This time around we actually played really well until the very end of the game. We should've killed them off and put the game out of sight. If you do that then you don't put yourself at risk of anything going wrong, but it only takes a second to score a goal and Everton made us pay with two in injury-time. After a goalless draw with Rangers we then let another two-goal lead slip at home to Liverpool. I was disappointed personally to concede a penalty in that one, but Berba really came to the rescue with a late winner to complete a brilliant hat-trick. We finished the month with three games away from Old Trafford, winning two and drawing one. Scunthorpe gave us an early fright in the Carling Cup before we fought back and convincingly went into the next round, then we had to settle for another point at Bolton – although it was a tough game and not that bad a result. The final game of the month was a great win at Valencia. That was when Chicha showed everyone what he could do on the big stage; scoring the winner straight after coming off the bench."

OCTOBER

Sat 2	Premier League
Sat 16	Premier League
Wed 20	Champions League
Sun 24	Premier League
Tue 26	Carling Cup 4th round
Sat 30	Premier League

October Stats

P:6	W:4	D:2	L:0
Scored: 10		Conceded: 5	
Clean Sheets: 3			

Events off the pitch took centre stage in October, but the Reds ended the month strongly – much to the delight of the ever-positive Patrice Evra...

“We knew we needed to start killing games off, but unfortunately we weren't able to do so against Sunderland or West Brom. When you are 2-0 up, like we were against West Brom, you should go on to win the game. If you make it 3-0 or 4-0 that makes it very difficult for other teams to come back. But when you keep things at the same tempo and it's still only 2-0, the opposition only need to score one goal to make things difficult for you. Everyone must take their share of the blame, not just the defence. For it to happen once is okay, but twice... I remember talking about the same thing after we played Liverpool in September saying I hope we don't give away a lead again, but we did it again. We knew we had two choices: to accept it or not accept it and that was the moment we had to make sure things changed. We pushed ourselves hard at the end of October and finished the month with four straight wins, despite it being a strange time around the club, with Wayne's contract situation. At that time some people said it was the end of the empire, but I always believed we could turn things around.”

NOVEMBER

Tue 2	Champions League
Sat 6	Premier League
Wed 10	Premier League
Sat 13	Premier League
Sat 20	Premier League
Wed 24	Champions League
Sat 27	Premier League
Tue 30	Carling Cup 5th round

November Stats

P:8	W:5	D:2	L:1
Scored: 17		Conceded: 8	
Clean Sheets: 4			

The Reds' grip on the Carling Cup was prised away by West Ham, but not before Chris Smalling and co had made impressive progress in the Premier League and Champions League...

"We were disrupted at the start of November when a virus spread through the squad. A couple of the lads had to stay behind in Manchester as we beat Bursaspor in Turkey, but not long after coming back we had maybe 10 or 12 players affected by it all. Even so, we just about managed to beat Wolves thanks to a brilliant late goal from Ji and that game summed up the never-say-die spirit at the club. It didn't take me long to realise that you never know when you're beaten when you're a United player. We just about got the majority of the players back for a pretty dull draw at City, before picking up a really exciting point at Villa. All the lads were disappointed afterwards, even though we'd scored twice in the last 10 minutes to draw the game, but the only real positive was that we'd managed to remain unbeaten. We felt in good shape in the title race and we still had plenty of players to come back, and we went joint top of the league by beating Wigan and then turned in an incredible display against Blackburn. Berba was untouchable that day and scored five goals, which shows you the talent the man has. Unfortunately our unbeaten run came to an end at West Ham in the Carling Cup, which sent us out of the competition and ended November on a bit of a low – but you can't dwell on results at this club, however good or bad they are."

DECEMBER

Tue 7	Champions League
Mon 13	Premier League
Sun 26	Premier League
Tue 28	Premier League

December Stats

P:4	W:2	D:2	L:0
Scored: 5		Conceded: 2	
Clean Sheets: 2			

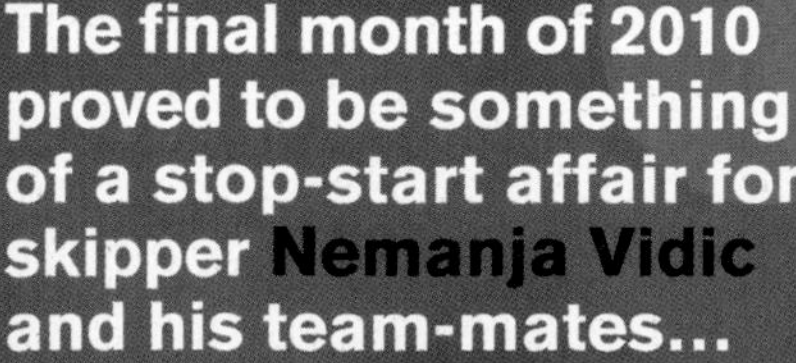

The final month of 2010 proved to be something of a stop-start affair for skipper Nemanja Vidic and his team-mates...

“We knew before the Blackburn game in November that we hadn't performed as well as we could, but from my experience Christmas is the time when we usually come into good form. We were a bit disappointed with the draw with Valencia in the Champions League because obviously we wanted to keep a clean sheet and become the first team to advance from the group stages without conceding a goal. But the most important thing was to finish where we wanted to, first in the group, and we did that. The win over Arsenal was a big result and it gave us a lot of confidence. We had to wait nearly two weeks to play our next game against Sunderland after the weather postponed our visits to Blackpool and Chelsea. It was strange to have so much time between matches - personally I always like to play and when you have that momentum you want to carry it on. On a personal note, being captain was a role I was really enjoying. It came as a bit of a surprise when the boss asked me but I was very proud. I didn't change anything in particular after becoming captain, but you have to think about your responsibilities – your behaviour, the way you play and the way you train. I knew that I needed to set a good example on and off the pitch. And ultimately I was determined to lead the team to more success.”

JANUARY

Sat 1	Premier League
Tue 4	Premier League
Sat 9	FA Cup 3rd round
Sun 16	Premier League
Sat 22	Premier League
Tue 25	Premier League
Sat 29	FA Cup 4th round

January Stats

P:7	W:6	D:1	L:0
Scored: 15		Conceded: 5	
Clean Sheets: 3			

United made an almost-perfect start to 2011, and Dimitar Berbatov was central to the Reds' success in an action-packed January...

"It was important to start the year by winning, and we managed to do that against West Brom and Stoke. Even if we weren't at our best, it was all about picking up those points to keep ourselves at the head of the table. We were in a good position when Liverpool came to Old Trafford in the FA Cup. I know they weren't happy about the penalty they conceded in the first minute, but it was definitely a foul by Daniel Agger on me. People know I don't go to ground easily! I thought we played very well and deserved to go through. We were steadily playing better and we defended brilliantly at Spurs before putting in another great display against Birmingham. It's always nice to score, so I was obviously delighted to get another hat-trick! I was playing with Wayne Rooney a lot and our partnership was working very well - when you speak the footballing language, you don't need to ask questions. You just need a quick glance at your partner to guess his plans. Then the Blackpool game – our game in hand on our rivals – was a huge result. We didn't play well until the last 20 minutes and then we came back to get a great win. Things were going very well for me personally but I was just taking each game as it came, just like the team."

FEBRUARY 2011

Tue 1	Premier League
Sat 5	Premier League
Sat 12	Premier League
Sat 19	FA Cup, Round 5
Wed 23	Champions League, 2nd round, 1st leg
Sat 26	Premier League

February Stats

P:6	W:4	D:1	L:1
Scored: 11		Conceded: 4	
Clean Sheets: 3			

The Reds' unbeaten league record came to an end at Molineux, but two victories over local rivals kept Darren Fletcher and the Reds in pole position in the title race...

"After starting the month off on a positive note with victory over Villa it was really disappointing to lose our unbeaten record in the league at Wolves. Ultimately though, our main concern was winning the league. We could remain unbeaten for the whole season and not win the title. What would be the point in that? We knew we had to bounce back and show our character and winning the Manchester derby was the perfect tonic. Wayne's winner was incredible, but it was the spirit we showed as a team that was pleasing. One man who epitomises the great Manchester United spirit is Gary Neville and we were all sad to hear him announce his retirement a few days before the derby. We followed up our win over City with a hard-fought victory over Crawley Town in the FA Cup and earned a decent draw away to Marseille. The victory at Wigan stretched our lead at the top to four points, but none of us were taking anything for granted. You have to earn the title. Nobody is going to give you the trophy lightly. We'd already seen how competitive the Premier League was getting with some shock results in the first half of the season. We knew we had to be wary of that and make sure we went into every game in top form because there was still plenty of hard work left to do."

MARCH

Tue 1 Premier League

Sun 6 Premier League

Sat 12 FA Cup quarter-final

Tue 15 Champions League, 2nd round, 2nd leg

Sat 19 Premier League

March Stats

P:5	W:3	D:0	L:2
Scored: 7		Conceded: 6	
Clean Sheets: 2			

United stuttered at Chelsea and Liverpool as springtime loomed, but the reaction of Wayne Rooney and his colleagues set up an impressive run of form...

"Obviously we weren't happy with losing back-to-back games at Stamford Bridge and Anfield, so it was really important to get back to winning ways against Arsenal – and we gave a really gritty performance. We knew they'd had a physical game against Barcelona earlier that week and with having some of our younger players in the side we knew if we could get about them we could tire them out. It was a case of trying to defend well, break quickly when we could and that proved to be the case. It was a great achievement to reach the FA Cup semi-finals, and we were delighted as well to get past Marseille in the Champions League. We knew from the first leg that they were a big, physical team and they made it difficult for us again at Old Trafford, but Chicha showed once again how dangerous he is in the box with both our goals. They got a late goal back but we managed to hold on and get the win we deserved. It's all about getting the job done when you get into the late stages of the season, and we managed to do that against Bolton at Old Trafford when Berba thankfully popped up with a late winner. That was a huge result; one which gave us that edge to keep pushing for the title."

APRIL

Sat 2 Premier League

Wed 6 Champions League Quarter-final, 1st leg

Sat 9 Premier League

Tue 12 Champions League Quarter-final, 2nd leg

Sat 16 FA Cup semi-final

Tues 19 Premier League

Sat 23 Premier League

Tues 26 Champions League Semi-final, 1st leg

April Stats			
P:8	W:6	D:1	L:1
Scored: 12		Conceded: 4	
Clean Sheets: 5			

Ryan Giggs continued to produce performances of enduring excellence throughout April amid the Reds' ongoing quest for silverware at home and abroad...

"We never give up. No matter what the score in the game is, we keep going, and the victory over West Ham felt like a really big result. We'd played some good stuff in the first half. We just gave silly goals away. We felt if we kept creating chances and got a goal back we could go on and win it. Wayne netted a fantastic hat-trick and scored another vital goal in our Champions League win at Chelsea. We had a good game plan and it was a top performance from the lads. Chelsea put us under pressure in the second leg at Old Trafford but we held firm. I played alongside Michael Carrick in the centre of midfield in both games and it's a role I really enjoyed. I think it's easier in there than out wide. On the wing you need to get up and down, whereas in midfield you can just pick your moments. Michael was in great form and when you've got the likes of Ji, Nani and Antonio outside you it makes our job a lot easier. Losing to City at Wembley was hard to take, but there's always another challenge around the corner and you have to move on. The late win over Everton was a crucial result and our great performance in Germany against Schalke meant confidence was sky high going into the final month of the season."

MAY

Sun 1	Premier League
Wed 4	Champions League
Sun 8	Premier League
Sat 14	Premier League
Sat 22	Premier League
Sat 28	Champions League

May Stats

P:6	W:3	D:1	L:2
Scored: 12		Conceded: 9	
Clean Sheets: 0			

Though the season ultimately ended on a low at Wembley, there was no disguising the achievement of Rio Ferdinand et al in clinching a 19th league title...

"Chelsea had put together a strong run of results to keep in touch with us, so when we lost at the Emirates without really performing, little doubts did start to creep in. The manager did a brilliant job, though, and made huge changes to the team to face Schalke, and his decision was vindicated by a great win which booked our place in the Champions League final and also allowed a few of us to recharge for the Chelsea game. We all knew how important that one was and we put in a brilliant performance. That game showed everyone that we were the best team in the country and deserved to win the league, which we confirmed with a hard-fought point at Blackburn. I've been fortunate enough to be part of squads that have won a few trophies, and you just really enjoy those moments. There was no time to dwell on winning the league because we had such a massive game to prepare for against Barcelona in the Champions League final at Wembley. We all wanted to give a better account of ourselves than we did against them in Rome two years earlier and, although we did, sadly I have to admit we lost to the better team. We believed we could beat them, but Barcelona are a great team who played really well on the night, and that's the level we have to aim for."

RED RECORD BREAKERS!

After securing the title at Ewood Park, Sir Alex and his players finally got their hands on the trophy on the final day of the season. Cue the Old Trafford party!

PREMIER LEAGUE
CHAMPIONS
BARCLAYS
BARCLAYS PREMIER LEAGUE

PLAYER PROFILES

TOMASZ KUSZCZAK

29

Born: 20 March 1982; Krosno Odrzanskie, Poland

Previous clubs: Hertha Berlin, West Bromwich Albion

Joined United: 10 August 2006

United debut: 17 September 2006 vs Arsenal (H), Premier League

International team: Poland

DID YOU KNOW? *Tomasz had an eventful United debut against Arsenal at Old Trafford. He conceded an early penalty but redeemed himself by saving the ensuing spot-kick from Gilberto Silva.*

BOSS SAYS: *"Tomasz is an excellent keeper. We can always rely on him to come in and do a job when we need him."*

ANDERS LINDEGAARD

Born: 13 April 1984; Dyrup, Denmark

Previous clubs: Odense Boldklub, Kolding FC (loan), Aalesunds FK

Joined United: 4 January 2011

United debut: 29 January 2011 vs Southampton (A), FA Cup

International team: Denmark

DID YOU KNOW? *It was the arrival of former Reds keeper Roy Carroll to Lindegaard's hometown club, Odense Boldklub, in 2009 which forced Anders' departure to Aalesunds FK where he excelled and caught the eye of United's scouts.*

BOSS SAYS: *"The challenge at Manchester United is always to look to the future and, in Anders, we have one of the brightest young goalkeepers in the game."*

BEN AMOS

Born: 10 April 1990; Macclesfield

Previous clubs: Trainee, Peterborough United (loan), Molde FK (loan), Oldham (loan)

Joined United: 1 July 2006

United debut: 23 September 2008 vs Middlesbrough (H), Carling Cup

International team: England (youth)

DID YOU KNOW? *Amos only became a goalkeeper by chance. He was a promising outfield player at Sunday League side Bollington United but, when their stopper failed to turn up, Ben went in goal due to his size and he never looked back!*

BOSS SAYS: *"Ben's a very promising young goalkeeper. He's very mature, level-headed and he has time on his side."*

PATRICE EVRA

Born: 15 May 1981; Dakar, Senegal

Previous clubs: Masala, Monza, Monaco

Joined United: 10 January 2006

United debut: 14 January 2006 vs Manchester City (A), Premier League

International team: France

DID YOU KNOW? *Pat can speak five different languages – French, English, Senegalese, Spanish and Italian. He is also learning Korean from his best friend Ji-sung Park.*

BOSS SAYS: *"To have played in almost every league game for the last two seasons is an astonishing achievement. Patrice comes into that category of being truly outstanding."*

RIO FERDINAND

05

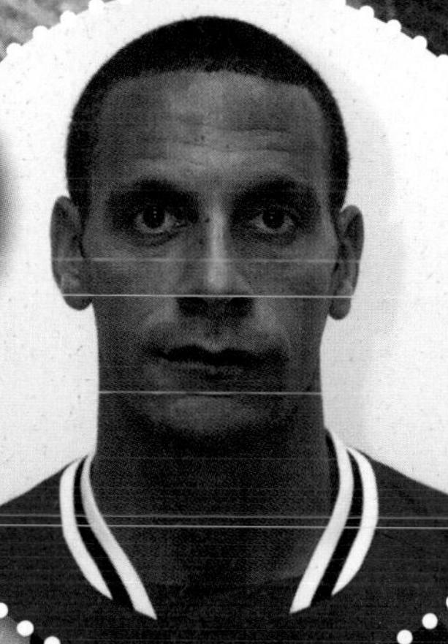

Born: 7 November 1978; Peckham

Previous clubs: West Ham, Bournemouth (loan), Leeds United

Joined United: 22 July 2002

United debut: 27 August 2002 vs Zalaegerszeg (H), UEFA Champions League

International team: England

DID YOU KNOW? *As well as his football career, Rio has a string of other interests. Aside from being the leading footballer on Twitter, he co-owns a restaurant and has his own online magazine, clothing line and music label, while he also runs his own charity.*

BOSS SAYS: *"We tried to bring Rio to the club when he was younger, but when we finally got him he matured into one of the best defenders in world football."*

JONNY EVANS

06

Born: 2 January 1988; Belfast, Northern Ireland

Previous clubs: Trainee, Royal Antwerp (loan), Sunderland (loan)

Joined United: 1 July 2004

United debut: 26 September 2007 vs Coventry City (H), League Cup

International team: Northern Ireland

DID YOU KNOW? *Jonny was one of four sets of siblings on United's books last season, until brother Corry joined Hull City on a permanent transfer. The other brothers are the Da Silva twins, the Keane twins and Wes and Reece Brown.*

BOSS SAYS: *"He's a wonderful, natural defender; a great reader of the game and he stood out as an accomplished player from a very young age."*

CHRIS SMALLING

12

Born: 22 November 1989; Greenwich

Previous clubs: Maidstone United, Fulham

Joined United: 7 July 2010

United debut: 8 August 2010 vs Chelsea (N), Community Shield

International team: England

DID YOU KNOW? *The defender is a talented tennis player and golfer and, as a youngster, he was a national judo champion having begun learning the sport from the age of six.*

BOSS SAYS: *"He is an extremely talented young defender. He's quick, strong and reads the game well. He's a great asset to the team."*

NEMANJA VIDIC

Born: 21 October 1981; Uzice, Serbia

Previous clubs: Red Star Belgrade, Spartak Moscow

Joined United: 5 January 2006

United debut: 25 January 2006 vs Blackburn Rovers (H), League Cup

International team: Serbia

DID YOU KNOW? *Vida, as he is known by his fellow players, grew up in Belgrade during wartime and had to prove that he was a footballer in order to be exempt from military service.*

BOSS SAYS: *"Nemanja was the obvious choice when we were deciding on a new captain to replace Gary Neville. He's fearless, a warrior and an extremely consistent performer."*

FABIO DA SILVA

Born: 9 July 1990; Rio de Janeiro, Brazil

Previous club: Fluminense

Joined United: 1 July 2008

United debut: 24 January 2009 vs Tottenham Hotspur (H), FA Cup

International team: Brazil (youth)

DID YOU KNOW? *Fabio was wrongly booked in United's Carling Cup win at Barnsley in October 2009 after referee Chris Foy got him mixed up with twin brother Rafael.*

BOSS SAYS: *"Fabio has made great strides forward in the last year and will make a fine Manchester United player in years to come."*

RAFAEL DA SILVA

Born: 9 July 1990; Rio de Janeiro, Brazil

Previous club: Fluminense

Joined United: 1 July 2008

United debut: 17 August 2008 vs Newcastle (H), Premier League

International team: Brazil (youth)

DID YOU KNOW? *Rafael and his brother Fabio are regularly mistaken for one another in the United dressing room. Sir Alex even began a dressing room discussion with Fabio for a poor performance, in the belief that he was Rafael!*

BOSS SAYS: *"Rafa has a wonderful enthusiasm for the game. His attitude and energy are terrific; he's like a rat up a drainpipe when he gets on the field."*

MIDFIELDERS

ANDERSON

Born: 13 April 1988; Porto Alegre, Brazil

Previous clubs: Gremio, FC Porto

Joined United: 1 July 2007

United debut: 1 September 2007 vs Sunderland (H), Premier League

International team: Brazil

DID YOU KNOW? *Anderson had to wait until September 2009 for his first United goal, but prior to that he had scored two vital penalties – the Reds' penultimate spot-kick in the 2008 Champions League final and the winning one in the 2009 Carling Cup final.*

BOSS SAYS: *"I think he can replace Paul Scholes. He's an outstanding talent with fantastic speed and strength and he's still only young."*

RYAN GIGGS

11

Born: 29 November 1973; Cardiff, Wales

Previous clubs: Trainee

Joined United: 9 July 1990

United debut: 2 March 1991 vs Everton (H), First Division

International team: Wales (retired)

DID YOU KNOW? *Ryan's all-time club appearances record rumbles on with no end in sight, but none of it might ever have happened – the winger trained with Manchester City as a schoolboy!*

BOSS SAYS: *"What more can you say about Ryan? He's a wonderful professional, he's always looked after himself in the right way and he's had an unbelievable career."*

JI-SUNG PARK

Born: 25 February 1981; Seoul, South Korea

Previous clubs: Kyoto Purple Sanga, PSV Eindhoven

Joined United: 8 July 2005

United debut: 9 August 2005 vs Debreceni (H), Champions League

International team: South Korea (retired)

DID YOU KNOW? *As a youngster, Ji was given boiled frog juice to drink by his parents in order to help him build up his strength as a footballer.*

BOSS SAYS: *"Ji has incredible energy and is also an extremely intelligent footballer. He is disciplined and capable of playing in a number of different positions."*

MICHAEL CARRICK

16

Born: 29 July 1981; Wallsend

Previous clubs: West Ham, Swindon (loan), Birmingham (loan), Tottenham Hotspur

Joined United: 31 July 2006

United debut: 23 August 2006 vs Charlton Athletic (A), Premier League

International team: England

DID YOU KNOW? As a youngster in his native South Shields, Michael represented Wallsend Boys Club – a fruitful supply of North East talent where Steve Bruce, Alan Shearer and Peter Beardsley all played as children.

BOSS SAYS: "Michael just goes about his job and rarely gives the ball away, which is a huge asset, and he's a really refined footballer who is a real United player."

NANI

17

Born: 17 November 1986; Praia, Cape Verde
Previous club: Sporting Lisbon
Joined United: 1 July 2007
United debut: 5 August 2007 vs Chelsea (N), Community Shield
International team: Portugal

DID YOU KNOW? *Nani isn't just good with his feet, he's also pretty useful with his hands as he proved on the team's 2009 pre-season tour when he played a Rihanna song on the piano for his team-mates.*

BOSS SAYS: *"The boy has matured into a top player. He can create goals and score goals and he has great ability with either foot."*

TOM CLEVERLEY

23

Born: 12 August 1989; Basingstoke
Previous clubs: Trainee, Leicester City (loan), Watford (loan), Wigan (loan)
Joined United: 1 July 2005
United debut: N/A
International team: England

DID YOU KNOW? A keen all-round sportsman, Tom is also an excellent snooker player and has turned down offers to play for amateur teams in his free time.

BOSS SAYS: "Tom's a real Manchester United-style player who wants to be on the ball all the time. He's got guts and bundles of energy, and those characteristics will serve him well."

DARREN FLETCHER

24

Born: 1 February 1984; Edinburgh, Scotland
Previous clubs: Trainee
Joined United: 3 July 2000
United debut: 12 March 2003 vs FC Basel (H), Champions League
International team: Scotland

DID YOU KNOW? Only Premier League rules prevented Fletch from making his United debut just after his 16th birthday. Because he was still only a schoolboy and not a trainee, he wasn't allowed to be named in the squad to face Aston Villa in 2000.

BOSS SAYS: "He's such a determined lad and a fantastic pro, but he's also an excellent player. He has incredible energy and has developed into a fine midfielder."

ANTONIO VALENCIA

25

Born: 4 August 1985; Lago Agrio, Ecuador
Previous clubs: El Nacional, Villarreal, Wigan
Joined United: 30 June 2009
United debut: 9 August 2009 v Chelsea (N), Community Shield
International team: Ecuador

DID YOU KNOW? Antonio became the first ever Ecuadorian footballer to win the Premier League when he helped United to Championship glory in 2010/11.

BOSS SAYS: "Antonio has been fantastic since he joined and he's improving all the time. He has great strength and balance, and his delivery into the box is first class."

DARRON GIBSON

28

Born: 25 October 1987; Derry, Northern Ireland
Previous clubs: Trainee, Royal Antwerp (loan), Wolves (loan)
Joined United: 1 July 2004
United debut: 26 October 2005 vs Barnet (H), League Cup
International team: Republic of Ireland

DID YOU KNOW? Gibson was part of the Reserves' Treble-winning squad in 2005/06, the season in which he was also awarded the prestigious Jimmy Murphy Young Player of the Year award.

BOSS SAYS: "Darron is the one player at our club who can always get a goal from outside the box; he's got tremendous shooting power."

STRIKERS

MICHAEL OWEN

07

Born: 14 December 1979; Chester

Previous clubs: Liverpool, Real Madrid, Newcastle United

Joined United: 3 July 2009

United debut: 9 August 2009 vs Chelsea (N), Community Shield

International team: England

DID YOU KNOW? *Owen is one of just four Englishmen – including Sir Bobby Charlton – who have won the prestigious European Footballer of the Year award, otherwise known as the 'Ballon d'Or'. Owen won it in 2001.*

BOSS SAYS: *"Michael is very clever in the last third. He knows when to time his runs and his finishing is excellent, he's just a natural goalscorer."*

DIMITAR BERBATOV

09

Born: 30 January 1981; Blagoevgrad, Bulgaria

Previous clubs: CSKA Sofia, Bayer Leverkusen, Tottenham

Joined United: 1 September 2008

United debut: 13 September 2008 vs Liverpool (A), Premier League

International team: Bulgaria (retired)

DID YOU KNOW? *In his spare time away from playing football, Dimitar is a keen and gifted artist who maintains he can draw 'anything he wants' freehand.*

BOSS SAYS: *"Dimitar is a genius. That's the only way to describe him at times. His vision is so good that he sees things other players couldn't even imagine."*

WAYNE ROONEY

Born: 24 October 1985; Liverpool

Previous club: Everton

Joined United: 31 August 2004

United debut: 28 September 2004 vs Fenerbahce (H), Champions League

International team: England

DID YOU KNOW? *Wayne Rooney was just 16-years-old when he scored his first Premier League goal - for Everton against Arsenal at Goodison Park. He scored his 100th against the same opposition in January 2010.*

BOSS SAYS: *"The term 'world-class' can be misused sometimes, but, when you see Wayne's performances, you know you're talking about a really world-class player."*

14

JAVIER HERNANDEZ

Born: 1 June 1988; Guadalajara, Mexico

Previous club: Chivas de Guadalajara

Joined United: 1 July 2010

United debut: 6 August 2010 vs Chelsea (N), Community Shield

International team: Mexico

DID YOU KNOW? *Chicharito, as the player is also known, is the third generation of his family to represent Mexico at a World Cup, following his grandfather in 1954 and his father in 1986.*

BOSS SAYS: *"He's a natural born finisher. Some players come alive in the penalty area and know exactly what to do to beat the goalkeeper. Javier is one of those strikers."*

DANNY WELBECK

Born: 26 November 1990; Manchester

Previous clubs: Trainee, Preston North End (loan), Sunderland (loan)

Joined United: 1 July 2007

United debut: 23 September 2008 vs Middlesbrough (H), League Cup

International team: England

DID YOU KNOW? *Danny has been playing for United since he was 11-years-old. He has risen through the club ranks and marked his Premier League debut against Stoke with a stunning goal in front of the Stretford End.*

BOSS SAYS: *"We see Danny as one of the great young players who have emerged from the academy. He will have a terrific career at the club."*

FEDERICO MACHEDA

Born: 22 August 1991; Rome, Italy
Previous clubs: Lazio, Sampdoria (loan)
Joined United: 1 September 2007
United debut: 5 April 2009 vs Aston Villa (H), Premier League
International team: Italy (under-21s)

DID YOU KNOW? *Kiko is United's youngest goalscorer in the Premier League era, after bagging a vital winner on his 2009 debut against Villa aged just 17 years and 224 days.*

BOSS SAYS: *"Since he arrived at the club, Kiko has progressed exceptionally well and we've been delighted with the player he has become – and there's still more to come."*

MAME BIRAM DIOUF

Born: 16 December 1987; Dakar, Senegal
Previous clubs: Diaraf, Molde FK, Blackburn (loan)
Joined United: 30 July 2009
United debut: 9 January 2010 v Birmingham (A), Premier League
International team: Senegal

DID YOU KNOW? *Diouf found the net on his Premier League debut for the Reds against Burnley, and also netted hat-tricks in his first games for United's Reserves and Blackburn Rovers, whom he joined on loan for the 2010/11 season.*

BOSS SAYS: *"He's quick, impressive in the air and a good striker of the ball. Overall, he's a really good centre-forward."*

PLAYER PROFILES

NEW ARRIVALS

With several experienced faces departing in the summer of 2011, Sir Alex Ferguson quickly snapped up some of the most promising young talents around...

PHIL JONES

BORN: 21 February 1992; Preston
PREVIOUS CLUBS: Blackburn Rovers
INTERNATIONAL TEAM: England

One of the hottest young talents in English football, Phil Jones was coveted by most of the Barclays Premier League's top clubs before United swooped to snap him up from Blackburn Rovers. The England Under-21 captain had demonstrated during the previous 18 months in Rovers' first team that he had the reading, judgement and physicality to cope with the rigours of top flight football, as well as the versatility to play in a defensive midfield role. Promisingly for United, Phil's impressive international partnership with new colleague Chris Smalling suggests the duo have a bright future for club and country.

ASHLEY YOUNG

BORN: 9 July 1985; Stevenage
PREVIOUS CLUBS: Watford, Aston Villa
INTERNATIONAL TEAM: England

One way of catching Sir Alex Ferguson's attention is to play well against United, and Ashley Young made a habit of doing that with both Watford and Aston Villa. The speedy winger shone for the latter in both meetings with the Reds last season; scoring a penalty at Villa Park and smashing a shot against the bar at Old Trafford. Comfortable on the left or right flank, Ashley has also demonstrated his growing versatility with impressive shifts in a central role, and his form has yielded regular involvement with the England national team.

DAVID DE GEA

BORN: 7 November 1990; Madrid, Spain
PREVIOUS CLUBS: Atletico Madrid
INTERNATIONAL TEAM: Spain (under-21s)

Replacing Edwin van der Sar is no mean feat, but United's search for a fitting successor to the Dutchman lasted well over a year, and the Reds finally settled on one of the most promising young goalkeepers on the continent. Blessed with excellent shot-stopping, distribution and organisation, David De Gea broke into the Atletico Madrid first team at the age of 18 and soon became a fixture between the sticks. For one so young he has amassed incredible experience; tasting success in Atletico's Europa League run of 2010 as well as Spain's triumph at 2011's European Under-21 Championships, and his signing represents a major coup for United.

TEAM-MATE TALES

Nani: Funniest, easiest to wind up, AND the loudest!

Fletcher: Best Trainer

CHRIS SMALLING

The Reds' defender only arrived at United in the summer of 2010, but it didn't take him long to figure out the workings of the Carrington dressing room...

BEST TRAINER
I'd say it's between Fletch or Giggsy. I'll go for Fletch – he's always so sharp.

WORST TRAINER
If he's not in the mood it has to be Ando. But when he's on it he can be sensational.

BEST DRESSED
I'd probably go for Rio. He wears some decent gear although his choice of footwear isn't always the best! Apart from that though he scrubs up pretty well.

WORST DRESSED
Ando – he's into his baggy shorts, and he has some crazy slippers that he likes to wear.

FUNNIEST
Nani. He's like a little kid some days and is always very happy. He really makes me laugh.

CLEVEREST
Vida. He's an intelligent guy. He's been to a lot of places in the world and is pretty knowledgeable on a range of different subjects.

TIDIEST
Hmmm....there are always a lot of boots all over the dressing room! I'll go for Antonio.

MOST RELAXED
Scholesy. He was always very laid back.

EASIEST TO WIND UP
Definitely Nani. He takes the bait very easily.

CHIEF PRANKSTER
Wazza. He's always up to something and you always have to keep an eye on him. I've been quite lucky and haven't had too many pranks played on me. My spot in the dressing room is tucked away in the corner so I'm not an easy target like some of the lads.

LOUDEST
Nani. He's always laughing, joking and shouting!

ANDERSON

The midfielder has often been labelled the worst dressed by his team-mates, but the Brazilian insists his casual look is simply misunderstood...

BEST TRAINER
It depends. Players can be different on different days. I'd probably say the twins, Ji-sung Park and Giggsy – they always train well.

WORST TRAINER
Again it depends. Sometimes it's me, other times it's someone else!

BEST DRESSED
Edwin [van der Sar] used to dress well. Patrice is up there, Rio is not bad... Michael Owen as well.

WORST DRESSED
It's definitely not me! I'm a relaxed guy, I like to wear flipflops, t-shirts and shorts. How everyone dresses depends on what the players are like. Some of the lads put on really smart clothes, but I go for a more relaxed and casual look.

FUNNIEST
It depends. Sometimes me, Nani, Patrice, Rio – everyone is always having fun and enjoying themselves.

CLEVEREST
Giggsy definitely.

BEST SINGER
Nobody! Actually Wazza is okay, but I'm really bad, I can't sing at all.

BEST DANCER
Me and Nani always enjoy dancing and I'd say Rio, Patrice and Wazza are pretty good too.

WORST DANCER
Probably Fletch and Michael Carrick.

BEST AT COMPUTER GAMES
I play a lot, so does Fabio and Rafa. On the football games I play as United or one of the Brazilian club teams.

BIGGEST JOKER
I always like to joke around with everyone even the boss! I concentrate when I'm on the pitch but off it I'm always laughing and joking. It's the way Brazilian people are.

Giggsy: Best trainer & smartest team-mate

Fabio & Rafa: Best at computer games

RED STARS

United's record-breaking 2010/11 campaign was a team effort, but two men stood out when it came to dishing out the personal awards at the club's annual Player of the Year ceremony...

Javier Hernandez
The Fans' Player of the Year

JAVIER HERNANDEZ

The Fans' Player of the Year

It was a debut season to remember for Chicha, who was named the Sir Matt Busby Player of the Year...

"I dreamt about playing for United for many years and it was a fantastic feeling when I first pulled on the shirt. I thought I'd play mainly with the Reserves during my first season with maybe a few minutes in the first team. But thanks to the boss and all my team-mates I played a little bit more!

"I still remember the first time I walked into the dressing room - all my team-mates and the staff made me feel so welcome and very comfortable. That made settling in much easier and it also really helped to have my family with me.

"To win the title in my first season was an unbelievable feeling. I knew all about the history of Manchester United when I joined and how important it is to win every tournament you play in, particularly the Premier League. I hope I can lift the trophy many more times in the coming seasons.

"The fans have helped me so much - even in my first game they sang my name. To win the supporters' award last season was very special and I'm very grateful to everyone that voted for me. It's amazing to see my name on the trophy alongside so many legends of the club. My aim now is just to keep improving and help the team achieve more success."

2010/11 Stats	
Appearances: 45	Goals: 20

They say...

"Chicha has set the world alight since he arrived. He works very hard and is always on the move, and he's a very intelligent player who is willing to work for the team."

MICHAEL CARRICK

"He's been phenomenal. It is not just his goals, but his movement, his all-round work ethic, his desire to be in the right positions and work hard. He is going to have a fantastic career."

RIO FERDINAND

"I must give Chicha great credit for the way he has taken to life at United. He doesn't only have great ability, he has real humility as well and that will take him far."

PATRICE EVRA

NANI
The Players' Player of the Year

The players' stand-out performer had defenders quaking in their boots, particularly during the first half of the campaign...

"To know that your team-mates have voted for you to win this award means a great deal. And I also have to thank them for the ways in which they have helped me improve.

"Last season was my most consistent for United. Every season I've been here I have improved and I was pleased with my performances last season – I created a lot of goals and scored more than the year before. I know I need to keep improving each year.

"The fans have been brilliant to me during my time here and I am very grateful for their support. Their backing gives me even more confidence to go out and perform to my best in every game.

"The challenge is always to improve every season. I know that's what the boss expects from me and I feel the same. I always expect a lot from myself and I know I have to work hard to achieve my goals. That's exactly what I plan to do."

2010/11 Stats	
Appearances: 49	Goals: 10

Nani
The Players' Player of the Year

They say...

"Nani was a real inspiration for us. Earlier on in the season when our form wasn't great he was winning us a lot of games and he was a constant threat."

DARREN FLETCHER

"He has all the qualities centre-backs hate coming up against. He's strong on the ball, he has great balance and really quick feet. He's a defender's worst nightmare."

CHRIS SMALLING

"Last season when we weren't playing our best football and having to grind out results, he was not only scoring goals, but making them as well."

RYAN GIGGS

Wayne Rooney
Goal of the Season

WAYNE ROONEY
Scorer of Goal of the Season

Once in a while as a United fan you get an 'I was there' moment. And on 12 February 2011, Wayne Rooney provided one when he fired home a stunning overhead kick to secure a vital win in the Manchester derby. There was only ever going to be one winner of United's Goal of the Season competition after that strike, described by his manager as "the best goal I've seen at Old Trafford."

"To score a goal like that in such a big game was a great feeling. It's something I'll never forget and it'll stay with me until the day I die," said Wayne after collecting his award. "You're always working on your technique, but goals like that are just instinctive. It's definitely one of the biggest buzzes I've felt after scoring."

BEHIND THE SCENES ON MATCHDAY

Getting Old Trafford ready for matchday is no mean feat. A cast of thousands are on hand to prepare the Theatre of Dreams for showtime, with plenty of work to be done before and after kick-off...

The first stadium safety checks start at 7am on matchday, no matter what time kick-off is. A 2,000-strong army of matchday staff ensures that every aspect of the ground is ready for the arrival of 76,000 fans. The turnstiles open – 90 minutes before kick-off – and safety staff in the Old Trafford control room, situated in the south-east corner of the ground, keep an eye on events. Over 100 internal and external CCTV cameras provide views of every car park, turnstile, exit gate and concourse, as well as Sir Matt Busby Way. The cameras can even monitor traffic several miles away on the M60, allowing staff to keeps tabs on the roads and pedestrian movements before and after games.

TURNSTILES E32 / E36

Ensuring the pitch is in peak condition is of paramount importance on matchday. Head groundsman Tony Sinclair and his team are the men charged with that task, part of which involves cutting the pitch three times on the day of the game, twice lengthways and once across at a length of 26mm. The line markings are then painted on with the pitch also watered prior to kick-off.

The players arrive at the stadium around two hours before kick-off, travelling by coach from the team hotel in the city centre. Once the squad have been briefed on their opponents, Sir Alex begins his team-talk and names his starting XI and substitutes. The dressing room is a hub of activity thereafter with Patrice Evra taking on the role of DJ. The Frenchman ensures his iPod is programmed with the perfect tunes to get the players suitably pumped up for the game. Goalkeeping coach Eric Steele and the 'keepers take to the field first to begin the warm-up, around 50 minutes before kick-off, with the outfield players joining them soon after. Those players not involved on the day watch the game from the directors' box.

Of course, with a worldwide fan base of millions, not every United fan can make it inside Old Trafford to see the Reds in action, or even to Manchester itself. The vast majority will tune in on TV – typically Sky Sports in England, while MUTV also provides exclusive behind-the-scenes news, views and match highlights, as well as live radio commentary of each game. On a day when a United game is being broadcast live to the masses, several outside broadcast (OB) trucks are stationed at Old Trafford with up to five miles of cable situated around the stadium. Each live game is assigned its own match director who has his or her own truck from which to view every image projected from numerous cameras and decide what the watching public will see. The TV commentators follow the match from their lofty perch in the commentary gantry, high up in South Stand, while the radio commentators and written press, including the club's official media team, are housed below them in the press box. After the game, the Man of the Match and both managers are interviewed in the tunnel.

The redevelopment of Old Trafford's quadrants, completed in August 2006, was a big step in the club's ongoing aim to hone one of world football's most iconic venues, increasing the capacity and also revolutionising United's matchday hospitality facilities. The Reds can now boast 8,000 executive hospitality seats, while another 2,000 hospitality seats are sold on a match-by-match basis. And, on occasion, fans within the suites are lucky enough to meet United legends and celebrity fans.

Hundreds of photographers are also on hand to capture every moment of matchday from Sir Alex meeting supporters to player and fan goal celebrations.

REDS ON PARADE!

The Reds took to the streets of Manchester in celebration of a record 19th title and, despite the rain, United fans were out in force to pay homage to their heroes...

CHAMPIONS
19
TIMES
19

BARCLAYS

SIR MATT BUSBY WAY

BARCLAYS

BARCLAYS

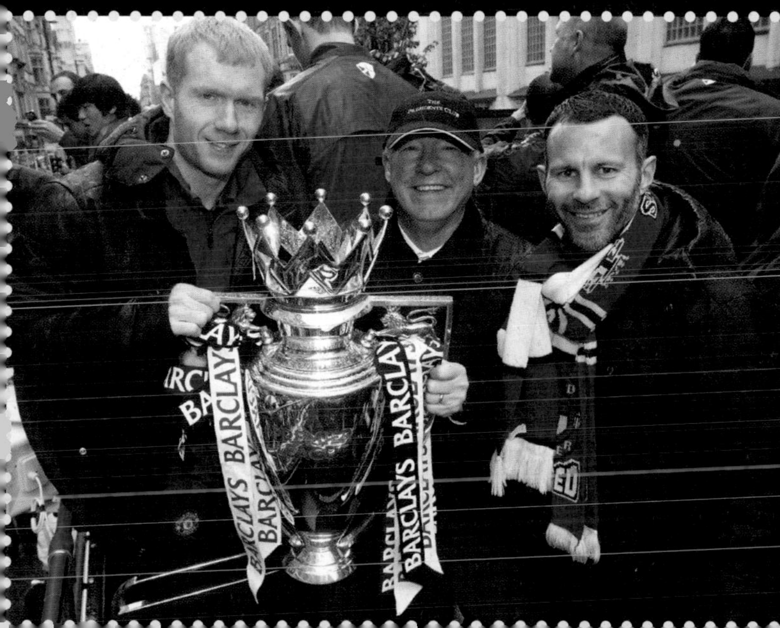
BARCLAYS

USA TOUR 2011
REDS GO STATESIDE!

United embarked on another trip to America in the summer of 2011 to continue preparations for the upcoming season. Sir Alex and his squad, including new arrivals Phil Jones, Ashley Young and David De Gea, stopped-off in Boston, Seattle, Chicago, New Jersey and Washington DC, securing five wins out of five during the three-week stay. It wasn't all work and no play for the Reds however, with a number of off-the-pitch activities factored into the team's hectic schedule, including a tour of Harvard University, a trip to the top of the famous Space Needle in Seattle and Empire State Building in New York, and a very special visit to The White House...

Rio & Kiko outside The White House

Vidic, Rio & Kasey Keller, Space Needle, Seattle

Sir Alex signs autographs

Park scores against MLS All-Stars

Henry & Owen on top of the Empire State Building, New York

Fabio gets to grips with a fish at Pike Place Market, Seattle

Our new signings pose in New Jersey

David Beckham with Rooney

Ando, Rooney & Nani celebrate against Chicago Fire

Ji tries his hand at making pizza in Chicago

2011 TOUR RESULTS

New England Revolution 1 United 4 *(Owen, Macheda 2, Park)*

Seattle Sounders 0 United 7 *(Owen, Diouf, Rooney 3, Park, Obertan)*

Chicago Fire 1 United 3 *(Rooney, Rafael Nani)*

MLS All-Stars 0 United 4 *(Anderson, Park, Berbatov, Welbeck)*

Barcelona 1 United 2 *(Nani, Owen)*

GARY NEVILLE TESTIMONIAL

Old Trafford paid tribute to one of its favourite sons at the end of the 2010/11 season, as Gary Neville brought down the curtain on his epic Reds career...

A homegrown veteran of 602 United appearances across almost 20 glorious years, Gary Neville earned legendary status at Old Trafford, and the Reds' former club captain was given a rousing send-off at the Theatre of Dreams in May 2011.

Seldom has the stadium's nickname seemed more apt. Neville admitted that after playing just once for United he could die happy, and to have been a cornerstone in the first team for over a decade was beyond the defender's wildest dreams.

He rose through the ranks as part of the famous Class of '92, which also spawned talents such as David Beckham, Paul Scholes, Nicky Butt and Phil Neville, who all donned the United shirt for the final time at Old Trafford as the Reds hosted Juventus in a special tribute match for Gary.

During the mid and late 1990s, the Italian giants were the toughest team that Neville and his colleagues came up against in European competition, which prompted their invitation back to M16 for the defender's final hurrah. They even acted as party-poopers by ensuring Gary finished his final game on the losing side.

Beckham, Giggs and Scholes were the stars of the show in the early exchanges; rolling back the years with some breathtaking individual skill, while huge cheers greeted Neville's every touch. The volume rose even further when Rooney slid home a finish from Giggs' cross, before the goalscorer and provider were withdrawn, along with Scholes, ahead of the looming Champions League final against Barcelona.

Steadily, Juventus grew into the game and drew level shortly before half-time when Simone Pepe converted Milos Krasic's cross with a powerful header. Late on during an evenly-contested second period, Manuel Giandonato curled in a magnificent free-kick to give the visitors victory.

The outcome mattered little, however. The highlight of the evening came when the star of the show was substituted late on, giving Old Trafford the chance to offer an outpouring of warmth and affection to one of its most dedicated servants. Gary Neville is a Red, the song goes. Few can boast such a deep hue of feeling and affection for United as its former captain.

THE TEAMS

Gary Neville Testimonial
Tuesday 24 May 2011, Old Trafford

MANCHESTER UNITED 1 *(Rooney 18)*
JUVENTUS 2 *(Pepe 40, Giandonato 78)*

United: Kuszczak (Lindegaard, 45); G Neville (Wootton, 85), Brown, O'Shea (Rafael, 65), P Neville; Beckham, Butt, Scholes (Gibson, 30), Giggs (Obertan, 30); Rooney (Bebe, 30), Owen (Anderson, 65). **Subs not used:** Fabio, Evans, Gill, Smalling, Fletcher.

Juventus: Storari (Manninger, 45); Motta (Marchisio 45), Chiellini (Bonucci, 45), Melo (Giandonato, 69), De Ceglie (Traore, 10); Pepe (Sorensen, 45), Krasic, Aquilani (Martinez, 45), Barzagli (Salihamidzic, 65); Toni (Matri, 45), Del Piero (Boniperti, 65). **Subs not used:** Buffon.

UNITED IN PRAISE

Some of Gary's former team-mates pay tribute to a true Reds legend...

"From the age of 18 right the way through to his 30s I don't think there were many better full-backs in world football."

MICHAEL OWEN

"The passion that he has is incredible. He's lived the dream to have played for so long for United. It's a privilege for anyone to play here, but when you've grown up as a fan, to play for the club is even better."

EDWIN VAN DER SAR

"Gary's just a winner. He played under some great leaders in Robbo, Brucey and Keaney, and by the time Roy left, Gary was ready to step up and become the leader of the football club."

DWIGHT YORKE

"When Gary came into the dressing room at 18 he seemed more like he was 38 – he already had plenty to say. His professionalism was outstanding. He was a great pro and a big character in the dressing room."

ROY KEANE

"He moaned for fun, but it was always for the right reasons and with everyone's interests at heart. He kept us on our toes. That made him fun to wind up of course but he always took it well."

ANDY COLE

THE LITTLE MASTER

Paul Scholes scored 150 goals before calling time on an epic United career. In tribute, we look back on 10 of the best from the Salford string-puller...

Chelsea 1 United 4, Premier League, 21 October 1995

Chelsea 1 United 4,

An absolutely stunning team goal which hinted at the collective brilliance of the Class of '92. Already a goal ahead through Scholes' early opener, United popped passes around with pace and purpose, all the while pulling Chelsea out of position. Then, when a killer pass finally put Scholes behind the ragged home defence, he advanced on goal and drilled home an unstoppable near-post finish.

Middlesbrough 3 United 4, Premier League, 10 April 2000

Bradford City 0 United 4,

On paper, it's a simple goal: chip it up for your mate to smash it in the back of the net. In actuality, Scholes' volley at Valley Parade needed unbelievable technique from both scorer and provider. David Beckham's marvellously flighted corner picked out the onrushing Scholes, and the midfielder's magnificent first time volley thundered into the bottom corner as players of both sides tried to get out of the way!

Middlesbrough 3 United 4,

Even the Boro fans found time to appreciate this unstoppable strike. Gary Neville received a short corner and teed up Scholes, 30 yards out. He raced onto the loose ball and belted it with an unbelievably crisp strike which scorched high into the Teessiders' goal, straight as an arrow.

United 3 Panathinaikos 1, Champions League, 21 November 2000

Newcastle 2 United 6,
Premier League, 12 April 2003

United 4 Blackburn Rovers 1,
Premier League, 31 March 2007

Newcastle 2 United 6,

Paul hit an immaculate hat-trick in one of United's best away performances under Sir Alex, but the outstanding goal of the bunch was his stunning second goal. A short corner was eventually ferried to him on the edge of the Newcastle area, and he needed no second invitation to blast an unstoppable drive high into Shay Given's top corner.

Aston Villa 0 United 3,

A goal becomes all the more satisfying when it crosses the line via the woodwork, so Scholesy's volley at Villa Park instantly took on iconic status. A half-cleared corner seemingly presented no danger as it dropped to the midfielder some 25 yards from goal, until he thundered a first-time effort into the roof of the net, via an almighty thud off the underside of Gabor Kiraly's crossbar. One of the sweetest hits you will ever see.

United 4 Blackburn Rovers 1,

One of the most important goals Scholes ever scored. United were trailing Blackburn in a key game during the title run-in, and Rovers were defending impeccably. No matter. Scholesy picked up possession just outside the area, jinked inside, shimmied past two challenges and drilled home a low finish. United went on to win and took the title.

United 1 Barcelona 0,

If you ask the man himself he'll claim that he mis-hit this shot. If true, it's the greatest shank in United's history! The semi-final tie was finely poised after a goalless first leg at the Nou Camp, but the Reds' midfield playmaker ensured progress to Moscow when he pounced on a poor clearance and sent a 25-yarder swerving into the top corner.

Manchester City 0 United 1,

Perhaps one of the most eagerly celebrated goals of Scholesy's epic haul. With United's title ambitions set to evaporate at the home of our noisy neighbours, the Reds summoned up the energy for one final push. Patrice Evra clipped a fine cross into the middle of the City area and there, unmarked, was the little maestro to direct home an inch-perfect header to send the travelling army wild – and secure a smacker from Gary Neville for Scholes!

United 3 Panathinaikos 1,

The ultimate team goal and regularly cited by Sir Alex as his favourite United goal of the last 25 years. Virtually every Reds player got a touch in an epic feat of keep-ball, before Teddy Sheringham's neat flick released Scholes on the edge of the area. The little maestro provided a fittingly deft finish to the move with a sublime chip over the visitors' goalkeeper.

Chelsea 0 United 3,

Trademark Scholes: the scorching long-ranger. Although quite how this goal managed to find its way through a cluster of defenders without a single touch is a mystery. Ryan Giggs outfoxed everyone by feinting to cross a free-kick and instead touched it to Scholes whose powerful drive - 30 yards from goal - almost tore through Carlo Cudicini's netting.

Few could have predicted the impact Alex Ferguson would make when he arrived at Old Trafford in November 1986. Having already broken up the Celtic-Rangers stranglehold on Scotland during his time at Aberdeen, he set his sights on domestic domination in England with the Reds.

Some 25 years and 36 trophies later, he is widely regarded as the greatest manager that has ever lived and he shows no signs of letting up just yet. Here we chart his tenure at Old Trafford to date...

Sir ALEX 25 YEARS

86: Arguably United's greatest ever signing as the b secure the services of Ferguson from Aberdeen on November.

87: The Reds finish in 11th place in the league, hile Ferguson completes the signings of Viv nderson, Brian McClair and Steve Bruce.

1988: United end the campaign as runners-up to Liverpool. Mark Hughes returns to OT after a two-year absence playing for Barcelona and Bayern Munich.

1989: Another 11th place finish for the Reds who also reach the FA Cup quarter-finals. Mike Phelan, Paul Ince, Neil Webb and Gary Pallister all join the club.

1990: Ferguson claims his first trophy – the FA Cup - as the Reds beat Crystal Palace in a replay at Wembley thanks to Lee Martin's winner.

1991: The United manager works his magic in Europe as he leads his team to glory in the Cup Winners' Cup. Two goals from Mark Hughes ensure victory over Barcelona in the final in Rotterdam. Later in the year, the Reds also win the UEFA Super Cup after beating Red Star Belgrade.

1992: The Reds snare another trophy – the League Cup, thanks to a 1-0 win over Sheffield Wednesday at Wembley. Some seven months later, the Boss pulls off a transfer masterstroke with the shock signing of Eric Cantona from Leeds for just £1.2million.

1993: United's 26-year wait for the title is finally over as the Reds are crowned inaugural Premier League champions. Soon after, Ferguson makes another inspired move in the transfer market with Roy Keane joining from Nottingham Forest.

1994: The Reds retain the league title and add the FA Cup to their collection with a 4-0 thrashing of Chelsea in the final to seal a first ever domestic Double for the club.

1995: After securing the services of Andy Cole from Newcastle, the Reds lose their talisman Cantona to an eight-month ban and suffer heartbreak on the final day of the league season and in the FA Cup final just days later.

1996: Having finished the previous season empty handed, the United manager sells a handful of major stars and replaces them with promising youngsters, who duly help a Cantona-inspired United win another domestic Double.

1997: It's a bittersweet end to the season for the Reds who secure another league championship, but are rocked by news of Cantona's retirement from football.

1998: United endure a rare barren season as Arsenal take advantage of an injury crisis at Old Trafford to overhaul a 12-point deficit and snatch the Premier League title.

1999: The greatest year in the club's history as United complete the Treble with a dramatic win over Bayern Munich. The Reds then become World Club Champions after beating Brazil's Palmeiras in Tokyo. Sir Alex is knighted for his services to football.

2000: There's no Treble hangover for the Reds who canter to title glory again, winning by an 18-point margin; a record in the Premier League era.

2001: United blow the opposition away once more as Sir Alex becomes the first manager in English football to win three titles in a row. Soon after, the Reds' boss announces he will retire at the end of the 2001/02 season.

2002: Sir Alex changes his mind about retiring and signs a new three-year deal, but United still end the campaign trophy-less as Arsenal reclaim the title at Old Trafford.

2003: The Reds' worst start to a Premier League campaign proves far from fatal when nine wins from the last 10 games leaves title-holders Arsenal trailing by five points. United sign an unknown winger from Sporting Lisbon by the name of Cristiano Ronaldo.

2004: Sir Alex claims a record fifth FA Cup but United lose the title to Arsenal, who remain unbeaten for the whole campaign. The Reds' response is to secure the services of Everton striker Wayne Rooney, who nets a stunning hat-trick on his debut.

2005: The season ends in heartbreak for the Reds who, having finished third in the league behind champions Chelsea and Arsenal, lose the FA Cup final on penalties to the Gunners despite dominating the game.

2006: The Reds win their second League Cup under Sir Alex, beating Wigan 4-0 at the Millennium Stadium. Chelsea again beat United to the title.

UNITED HONOURS UNDER SIR ALEX*

- League Championship: 12
- Champions League: 2
- European Cup Winners' Cup: 1
- FA Cup: 5
- League Cup: 4
- FIFA Club World Cup: 1
- Intercontinental Cup: 1
- UEFA Super Cup: 1
- Charity/Community Shield: 10

*Correct at 30 August 2011

2007: With Rooney and Ronaldo in inspired form, Sir Alex and his men regain their grip on the Premier League trophy, denying Chelsea a third straight crown, though the Blues do deny United the Double with victory in the first FA Cup final at the newly built Wembley Stadium.

2008: Ronaldo's 42-goal haul helps secure a last-day title triumph before United complete the double with a dramatic penalty shoot-out victory over Chelsea in the Champions League final. United are also crowned world champions after winning the Club World Cup in Japan.

2009: The Reds see off a late surge from arch rivals Liverpool to win another hat-trick of titles, while Sir Alex adds a further League Cup to his trophy tally after his side beat Spurs.

2010: Chelsea deny United a historic fourth straight title after taking the Premier League title by a solitary point, but the Reds hold on to the League Cup after victory over Villa.

2011: United become the most successful club in English football after winning a record 19th title - the perfect way for the boss to mark 25 years at Old Trafford.

YOUNG ENTERPRISE

United's rich history in the FA Youth Cup continued with a record-extending 10th competition triumph in 2011. Here's how the young Reds made history...

3rd round – 10 January 2011
United 3 Portsmouth 2
(Pogba, Fry o.g, W. Keane)

Paul McGuinness' youngsters roared into a three-goal lead through Paul Pogba's long-range scorcher, an own-goal by Pompey goalkeeper Tom Fry and a clinical finish from striker Will Keane. The visitors finished strongly and pulled back two late goals, but United hung on.

4th round – 19 January 2011
West Ham 0 United 1
(W. Keane)

A hard-fought game on a freezing night at Upton Park was settled by a poacher's goal from Will Keane. Larnell Cole's inventive set and volley was too hot for Hammers goalkeeper Sam Cowler to handle, and Keane nipped in to head home the rebound and take the Reds through.

5th round – 16 February 2011
United 1 Newcastle 0
(Morrison)

An injury-hit United side created and passed up a string of opportunities, but progress was secured midway through the second half when Ravel Morrison picked his way through the Magpies' defence and blasted home a finish via the underside of the visitors' crossbar.

6th round – 13 March 2011
Liverpool 2 United 3
(Cole pen, Morrison 2)

What a comeback! United looked set to exit the competition after falling two goals behind and losing Paul Pogba to a controversial red card, but Larnell Cole began the fightback with a penalty before Ravel Morrison slotted home an equaliser and volleyed in a spectacular winner.

Semi-final – 10 & 20 April 2011
Chelsea 3 United 2
(Lingard, Pogba)

United 4 Chelsea 0
(Morrison, W. Keane 3 (1 pen))

An absorbing semi-final tie pitted the Reds against the reigning FA Youth Cup holders. The Blues deservedly edged the first leg with a 3-2 win at Stamford Bridge in which Jesse Lingard and Paul Pogba struck to keep the Reds in the tie, before Paul McGuinness' side turned on the style at Old Trafford in the second leg. Ravel Morrison's deflected opener levelled the tie, before Will Keane's poached hat-trick ensured emphatic progress to the final.

Final – 17 & 23 May 2011
Sheffield United 2 United 2
(Lingard, W. Keane)

United 4 Sheffield United 1
(Morrison 2, W. Keane 2 (1pen))

The Reds were twice pegged back at Bramall Lane after taking leads through Jesse Lingard and Will Keane, but another swaggering home performance ensured the silverware returned to the Old Trafford museum. Ravel Morrison opened the scoring with a calm finish, before Will Keane stroked home a clinical penalty just before the interval. Morrison hammered home another midway through the second period and, although the visitors pulled a goal back, Keane had the final say with another unstoppable finish to wrap up a hugely successful campaign for Paul McGuinness' talented young crop.

REDS IN TRAINING

Spot the Difference

Can you spot the 7 differences between the two celebration photographs?

Answers on Page 60

Guess Who?

Can you work out who the 2 Reds are in these photos?

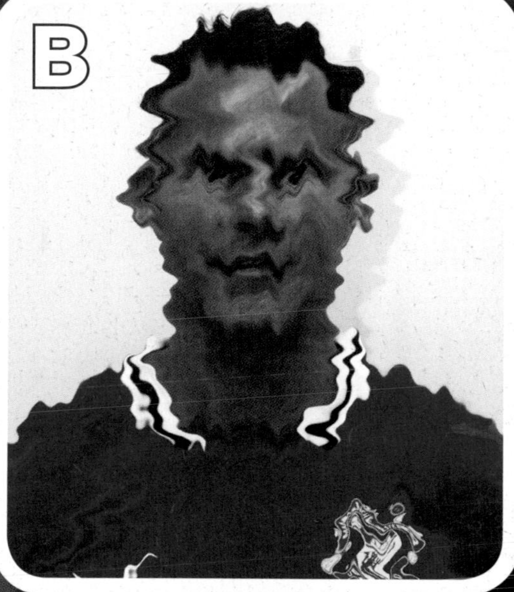

Answers on Page 60

True or False?

How much do you know about your Red heroes?
Put your knowledge to the test...

1. Ryan Giggs made his United debut against Manchester City back in 1991.
2. Sir Alex Ferguson has won the FA Cup a record five times.
3. United won the Treble in 1999 on what would have been Sir Matt Busby's 90th birthday.
4. Nemanja Vidic is older than Patrice Evra.
5. Sir Bobby Charlton is United's all-time top goalscorer.

Answers on Page 60

Wordsearch

The players can pick out a team-mate in a crowded penalty box, but do you have the same vision?

Hidden in the wordsearch below are the surnames of 10 United legends.

Can you find them? Words can go horizontally, vertically, diagonally and backwards.

F	N	V	X	T	C	P	A	W	R	Q
S	S	O	D	L	A	N	O	R	A	X
E	T	O	V	L	O	D	Y	M	J	L
L	L	M	L	T	Y	R	A	F	R	H
O	M	C	N	S	O	H	W	T	O	C
H	W	A	N	O	K	H	K	Z	B	C
C	C	D	N	C	T	J	L	P	S	N
S	Q	E	E	G	S	G	A	R	O	X
Q	Y	B	F	M	E	M	V	E	N	W
D	R	X	N	N	B	F	H	Y	R	K
C	H	A	R	L	T	O	N	P	Z	P

BEST, CANTONA, CHARLTON, SOLSKJAER, ROBSON,

ROONEY, RONALDO, LAW, SCHOLES, BECKHAM

Answers on Page 61

Spot the Real Ball!

Can you guess which is the real ball in this photograph as Fabio battles to win possession with Fernando Torres?

Answers on Page 61

Anagrams

Unscramble the anagrams below to reveal the names of 10 United stars...

1. **Radar Leading Ends**
2. **Help Joins**
3. **Vicar Repeat**
4. **Advice Jam Inn**
5. **Radar Hen Jive Zen**
6. **Bail Diva Sofa**
7. **Prank Jig Us**
8. **Whale Income**
9. **Crack Hail Crime**
10. **Earn Nods**

Answers on Page 61

Who's Going to Score?

Chicharito, Michael Owen and Wayne Rooney have the goal in their sights, but only one player can make it through the opposition's defences – can you work out who will score?

Answers on Page 61

United Quiz

1 By how many points did the Reds win the 2010/11 title?

2 At what ground did United clinch the championship crown?

3 What shirt number does Javier Hernandez wear?

4 Who scored more goals last season – Hernandez or Dimitar Berbatov?

5 In what year did Antonio Valencia join United?

6 Which team did the Ecuadorian make his debut against?

7 How many goals did Paul Scholes score for United?

8 Who played more games for the club – Scholes or Gary Neville?

9 Who did United beat to win the 2011 Community Shield?

10 What nationality is Anders Lindegaard?

11 In what month and year did Sir Alex Ferguson take over at Old Trafford?

12 What was the first trophy the Boss won with United?

13 Rooney netted the Reds' 2010/11 Goal of the Season with a stunning overhead kick against Manchester City – what was the final score in that game?

14 Who did Nemanja Vidic score his first ever United goal against?

15 How many goals did Vidic score last season?

16 Who is older – Michael Carrick or Ji-sung Park?

17 Name the Reds' first team fitness coach.

18 From which club did Chris Smalling join United?

19 Against whom did Smalling net his first goal?

20 Who scored United's final goal of the 2010/11 campaign?

Answers on Page 61

Quiz Answers:

Spot the Difference, Page 54

Guess Who?, Page 55

Fabio

Ryan Giggs

True or False?, Page 55

1 FALSE
It was against Everton in March 1991.

2 TRUE
1990, 1994, 1996, 1999, 2004

3 TRUE
26 May 1999

4 FALSE
Patrice was born on 15 May 1981, Nemanja on 21 October 1981.

5 TRUE
The United legend has 249 goals to his name.

Wordsearch, Page 56

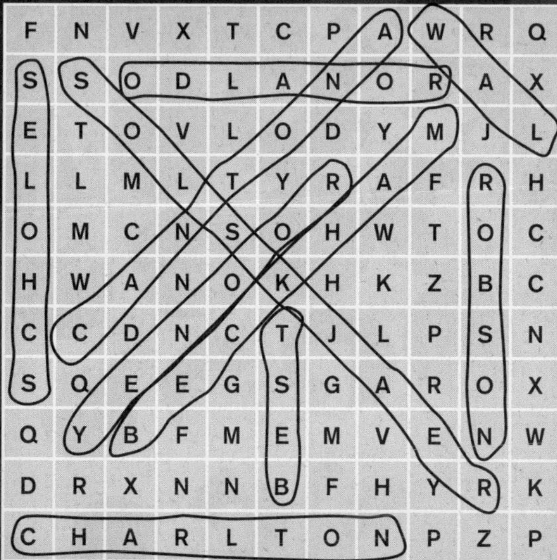

Spot the Real Ball, Page 57

Anagrams, Page 57

1 Anders Lindegaard
2 Phil Jones
3 Patrice Evra
4 Nemanja Vidic
5 Javier Hernandez
6 Fabio da Silva
7 Ji-sung Park
8 Michael Owen
9 Michael Carrick
10 Anderson

Who's Going to Score?, Page 58

Wayne Rooney scored!

United Quiz, Page 59

1 Nine points

2 Blackburn's Ewood Park

3 No.14

4 Berbatov

5 2009

6 Chelsea in the 2009 Community Shield

7 150

8 Scholes - 676

9 Manchester City

10 Danish

11 November 1986

12 1990 FA Cup

13 2-1 to United

14 Wigan

15 Five

16 Park

17 Tony Strudwick

18 Fulham

19 Scunthorpe

20 Wayne Rooney v Barcelona

Where's Fred the Red?

Can you spot Fred in the picture below?

MANUTD.COM